P9-BJB-778

DISCARD

CAREER EXPLORATION

Mechanical Drafter

by Rosemary Wallner

Consultant:
American Design Drafting Association

CAPSTONE BOOKS

an imprint of Capstone Press
Mankato, Minnesota

103923

Capstone Books are published by Capstone Press
P.O. Box 669, 151 Good Counsel Drive, Mankato, Minnesota 56002
http://www.capstone-press.com

Copyright © 2000 Capstone Press. All rights reserved.
No part of this book may be reproduced without written permission from the publisher.
The publisher takes no responsibility for the use of any of the materials or methods
described in this book, nor for the products thereof.
Printed in the United States of America.

Library of Congress Cataloging-in-Publication Data
Wallner, Rosemary, 1964–
    Mechanical drafter/by Rosemary Wallner.
    p. cm.—(Career exploration)
    Includes bibliographical references and index.
    Summary: Introduces the career of mechanical drafter, discussing educational
requirements, duties, workplace, salary, employment outlook, and possible
future positions.
    ISBN 0-7368-0331-9
    1. Mechanical drawing—Vocational guidance—Juvenile literature.
2. Drafters—Vocational guidance—Juvenile literature. [1. Mechanical drawing—
Vocational guidance. 2. Occupations. 3. Vocational guidance.] I. Title. II. Series.
T357 .W28 2000
604.2'023—dc21   99-23534
                                                   CIP

Editorial Credits
Leah K. Pockrandt, editor; Steve Christensen, cover designer; Kia Bielke, illustrator;
    Heidi Schoof, photo researcher

Photo Credits
FPG International LLC, 20, 25
Gregg R. Andersen, cover, 6, 16, 35, 36, 43, 47
Hewlett-Packard Company, 10, 22
Index Stock Imagery, 39
Integraph Computer Systems, 13
International Stock/Chuck Mason, 9; James David, 14; Giovanni Lunardi, 18
Photo Network/Bill Bachmann, 33
Uniphoto/Llewellyn, 26; Uniphoto, 40
Visuals Unlimited/Jeff Greenberg, 30

Table of Contents

Chapter 1 Mechanical Drafter 7

Chapter 2 A Day on the Job 15

Chapter 3 The Right Candidate............... 23

Chapter 4 Preparing for the Career 31

Chapter 5 The Market 37

Fast Facts 4

Skills Chart.. 28

Words to Know................................... 42

To Learn More.................................... 44

Useful Addresses 45

Internet Sites................................... 46

Index 48

Fast Facts

Career Title	Mechanical Drafter
O*NET Number	22514D
DOT Cluster (Dictionary of Occupational Titles)	Professional, technical, and managerial occupations
DOT Number	007-281-010
GOE Number (Guide for Occupational Exploration)	05.03.02
NOC Number (National Occupational Classification-Canada)	2253
Salary Range (U.S. Bureau of Labor Statistics and Human Resources Development Canada, late 1990s figures)	U.S.: $19,000 to $50,750 Canada: $22,600 to $56,600 (Canadian dollars)
Minimum Educational Requirements	U.S.: associate's degree Canada: diploma
Certification Requirements	U.S.: optional Canada: optional

Subject Knowledge

Computers and electronics; engineering and technology; design; mathematics; physics; fine arts

Personal Abilities/Skills

Use geometry and other kinds of higher mathematics; use clear language to write technical reports; perform detail work with great accuracy; use fingers skillfully; make finger and hand movements correspond with seeing to operate equipment; adjust instruments; use pen to make sketches; use measuring tools

Job Outlook

U.S.: average growth
Canada: fair

Personal Interests

Mechanical: interest in applying mechanical principles to practical situations, using machines, hand tools, or techniques

Similar Types of Jobs

Heating ventilation and air conditioning drafter; piping drafter; machine drafter; fire protection drafter; instrumentation drafter; architectural drafter; electrical drafter; product drafter; general drafter; civil drafter; cartographer; landscape drafter; marine drafter; structural drafter

Chapter 1

Mechanical Drafter

Mechanical drafters make detailed drawings of machines and other products. Their drawings provide visual direction for making these products. Drafters show exact details of products on their drawings. These details include product sizes and building materials needed. The details also include the necessary instructions to make the products.

Defining the Career

Mechanical drafters have a variety of career choices. Many mechanical drafters work for manufacturing companies. These companies build machines and products such as desks, lamps, telephones, cars, and skateboards. These companies produce these machines and products for customers such as stores and car dealerships.

Mechanical drafters make detailed drawings of machines and other products.

Mechanical drafters make the drawings that describe how to properly manufacture products. These drawings describe the objects' sizes and shapes completely and accurately. These drawings are sometimes called layouts. Workers who make the products use drafters' drawings.

Mechanical drafters assist other engineers in designing systems that produce products that people use every day. These products include such things as soap and frozen food.

Other types of mechanical drafters work in the architectural industry. These drafters support engineers in architectural engineering and construction. Architectural engineers help design structures such as buildings. Some mechanical drafters help design heating ventilation and air conditioning (HVAC) systems. They also help design plumbing systems.

Defining the Job

Mechanical drafters work as a part of teams. They usually work with mechanical engineers, designers, and other drafters. Designers create the overall look of products or machines. Mechanical engineers have more education than mechanical drafters do. Engineers are trained to understand all aspects of product

Mechanical drafters make product drawings.

design. Engineers on teams often are called project engineers. Mechanical drafters sometimes are called mechanical design technicians.

Mechanical engineers often meet with customers. They find out what machines or other products customers need. Engineers write down the details of these products. Engineers often draw rough sketches to show their concepts to drafters.

Mechanical drafters then meet with the engineers to look at the list of details and sketches. They may ask questions about making the items.

Mechanical drafters' drawings show front, top, and side views of machines or other products.

Drafters are trained to understand and follow engineers' instructions. Drafters also may use customers' ideas when they make their drawings.

The Drafting Process

Mechanical drafters use many methods to help others understand their drawings. Mechanical drafters draw thick lines to show the main shape of products. Drafters draw thin lines to show additional details such as centerlines of holes.

They use various types of lines and special symbols to show the products' details.

Mechanical drafters do other things to add meaning to their drawings. They draw the front, top, and side views of machines or products. These drawings show all dimensions of the individual parts of these objects. Dimensions include width, height, and depth.

Mechanical drafters include other information in their drawings. For example, they indicate what materials to use to build the machines or products. These materials may include metal, plastic, glass, or wood. Drawings also list step-by-step instructions so manufacturers will know how to build the objects.

Senior drafters or designers check mechanical drafters' drawings. These senior drafters or designers check the dimensions, proposed materials, and instructions. They make sure the drawings include all necessary information. The original drafters may then have to correct their drawings. Drafters make sure the details on their drawings are accurate and complete.

Mechanical drafters show their drawings to their project engineers and customers after they make final changes. Drafters answer questions from engineers and customers about their drawings. They sometimes must change parts of the drawings that are unclear to engineers or customers.

Equipment

In the past, mechanical drafters used different tools than they use today. They used pens, pencils, and a variety of papers to draw their plans.

Today, nearly all mechanical drafters use computer systems to create their drawings. These systems are called Computer-Assisted Drafting or Computer-Aided Drafting (CAD) workstations. These systems also may be called Computer-Aided Drafting and Design (CADD) or Computer-Assisted Engineering (CAE). In Canada, mechanical drafters often are called CAD operators.

Mechanical drafters using CAD systems make their drawings with a computer mouse and keyboard. As drafters draw, computer monitors display their plans. Drafters use computer programs to turn their drawings and see them from all views. The drawings can be stored electronically on disks or computers. This storage makes it easy for drafters to change or copy drawings.

The CAD System

Mechanical drafters began using Computer-Assisted or Computer-Aided Drafting (CAD) systems in the 1970s. Computers and computer programs have greatly changed and improved since then.

Mechanical drafters who work with CAD systems use computers to produce their drawings. The images appear on computer monitors and may be printed on different sizes of paper.

Mechanical drafters print out their drawings using a large printer called a plotter. Drafters produce drawings in either inches or millimeters. In inches, drawing sizes range from 8.5 by 11 inches to 34 by 44 inches. In millimeters, drawing sizes range from 210 by 297 millimeters to 841 by 1,189 millimeters.

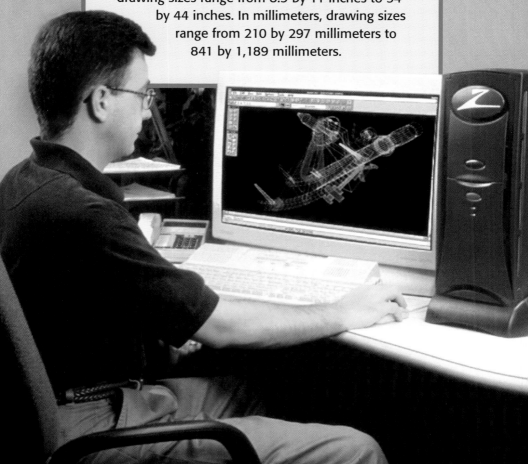

Chapter 2

A Day on the Job

Mechanical drafters work in a variety of office settings. Mechanical drafters who make drawings by hand sit at large drawing boards or tables. Drafters using CAD systems sit at computer workstations. Some drafters have their own office spaces called cubicles. These small work areas have movable walls or panels. Some drafters work in large rooms with other drafters.

Drafting Duties

Mechanical drafters have various job responsibilities. Managers or supervisors assign tasks to drafters. Drafting supervisors guide drafters through their jobs. They also answer any questions drafters may have. This guidance helps drafters keep projects on schedule.

Drafting supervisors guide drafters through their jobs.

Mechanical drafters' drawings are plotted on large sheets of paper.

Mechanical drafters sometimes use calculators and technical handbooks to establish design details. They decide on the designs' exact dimensions.

Mechanical drafters make lists of materials needed for construction of the items. The finished drawings are printed on large sheets of paper with printers called plotters. These finished drawings also are called prints.

Checkers examine the drawings. These people examine all the calculations for errors. Checkers also make sure design dimensions and specifications are correct. Mechanical drafters use the checkers' markings to make corrections to the drawings.

Mechanical Drafters on the Job

Mechanical drafters' daily duties vary with their assorted tasks. A mechanical drafter's workday often includes meetings. These meetings may concern the progress of product designs in preparation for a customer review.

Mechanical drafters are expected to make review copies of their designs. Lead engineers and project managers check these drawings. Reviews allow drafters to estimate what percentage of the designs need to be completed. Reviews also allow mechanical drafters to discuss any problems that may occur. Drafters also may attend customer meetings to explain their designs and answer customers' questions.

Mechanical drafters work in a variety of industries.

Mechanical drafters may attend other types of meetings. Material suppliers often show the latest technology used in mechanical drafting at meetings. This technology could include electrical switches, plastics, pumps, or motors.

Mechanical drafters normally work 40 hours per week. They sometimes must work additional hours. Employers may ask mechanical drafters to assist with high priority assignments. Drafters are expected to work extra hours to complete the assigned work. They may earn extra money for working these extra hours.

Job Levels

Mechanical drafters work their way through different job levels in companies. Level 1 jobs are entry-level positions for people with basic drafting training or limited experience. Level 1 drafters copy sketches and drawings prepared by other drafters.

Level 2 drafters have some specialized technical drafting or engineering skills. These drafters also have some experience in the field. Mechanical drafters with an associate's degree may begin work as Level 2 drafters. Students earn an associate's degree at a technical and vocational school or community college. It normally takes students about two years to earn an associate's degree. Level 2 drafters copy plans and make simple drawings.

Level 3 and Level 4 positions are for experienced drafters. These drafters create

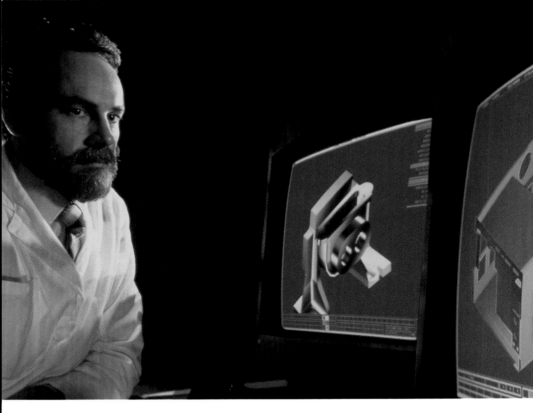

Mechanical drafters design products and machines used to make products.

their own drawings. They may work by themselves with direction from supervisors. They may recommend minor design changes to project engineers or managers. They also help direct less experienced drafters.

Drafting supervisors occupy the highest level of drafting positions. They oversee

20

the work of other drafters. Supervisors create time schedules. They make sure work is completed on time. Supervisors also assign work to each drafter.

Specialty Areas

Mechanical drafters work for different types of companies and businesses. Some mechanical drafters work on the designs of new products. Such products include air conditioners, furnaces, computer printers, and copy machines. These drafters work with designers and engineers. Drafters make drawings based on designers' ideas and engineers' guidelines.

Mechanical drafters work in a variety of industries. Mechanical drafters may work in the plastics industry. Some mechanical drafters design the plastic that packaging products are sold in. Other drafters work in plastics plants that make molded parts. These parts include computer casings, storage containers, and utensils. Drafters may design both the products and the machinery used to make the products.

Chapter 3

The Right Candidate

Mechanical drafters need a variety of skills and interests. They should be creative, imaginative, and persistent. A persistent person keeps doing something in spite of challenges. Drafters also must be organized, accurate, and detail-oriented.

Abilities and Interests

Mechanical drafters need to know a great deal about machines and other products. They also must know about computers and other devices used with computers. These include plotters, printers, and electronic file storage systems. Drafters are able to save large computer files on these systems instead of on their computers.

Mechanical drafters need a variety of skills. They must be able to envision the items they are drawing in two and three dimensions. A

Mechanical drafters should be interested in computers.

23

two-dimensional drawing is a flat drawing that shows the height and width of the design. A three-dimensional drawing shows the height, width, and depth of the design. Depth makes different objects in a drawing appear to be closer or farther away from the viewer. A three-dimensional drawing seems more realistic than a two-dimensional drawing.

Mechanical drafters must have good eyesight and hand control. Drafters perform detailed work. They must be able to sketch freehand. Even drafters who work on computers must be able to make good sketches by hand. Drafters must be able to keep their hands steady while drawing.

Mechanical drafters must be organized. During a week, they may work on several projects. They need to keep all their work on schedule. They must work quickly and accurately.

Mechanical drafters must have good communication skills. They may need to talk

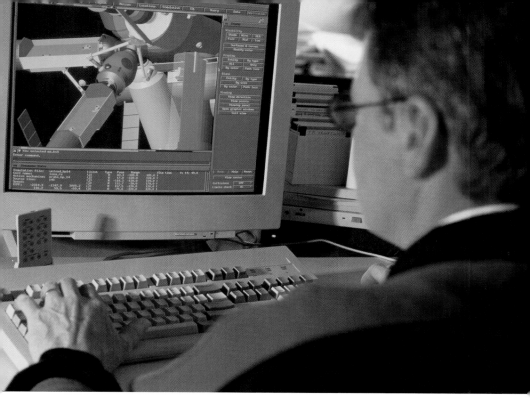

Mechanical drafters must be able to work quickly and accurately.

and write letters to engineers, customers, and other drafters. They need to write down exact steps for making machines or products. These steps help others assemble the objects. Mechanical drafters also need to listen well. They need to understand and follow directions.

Mechanical drafters often are part of design teams. They must work well with others.

Work Styles

Mechanical drafters must be neat and accurate. They must try to have very few errors in their drawings. Supervisors check drawings to be sure that errors are corrected before others use the drawings.

Mechanical drafters must be patient and persistent. They often must work many hours on one project. Drafters should be able to work on projects until they are completed.

Mechanical drafters must work well with others. They often are part of design teams. Drafters in large companies may work with 80 or more people.

Mechanical drafters need concentration skills. They often work many hours on detailed drawings. Drafters must concentrate on their tasks. They must check and recheck their work for errors.

Mechanical drafters also need to be able to handle stress. They must get projects done on time. It may be stressful to keep several projects on schedule.

Basic Skills

Mechanical drafters need math, drafting, English, and science skills. Mechanical drafters compute the correct dimensions for their designs. They make drawings according to engineers' instructions. They

Skills

Workplace Skills   Yes / No

Resources:
Assign use of time . . . . ✓ ☐
Assign use of money . . . . ✓ ☐
Assign use of material and facility resources . . . . ✓ ☐
Assign use of human resources . . . . ✓ ☐

Interpersonal Skills:
Take part as a member of a team . . . . ✓ ☐
Teach others . . . . ✓ ☐
Serve clients/customers . . . . ✓ ☐
Show leadership . . . . ✓ ☐
Work with others to arrive at a decision . . . . . ✓ ☐
Work with a variety of people . . . . ✓ ☐

Information:
Acquire and judge information . . . . ✓ ☐
Understand and follow legal requirements . . . . ✓ ☐
Organize and maintain information . . . . . . ✓ ☐
Understand and communicate information . . . . ✓ ☐
Use computers to process information . . . . . ✓ ☐

Systems:
Identify, understand, and work with systems . . . . ✓ ☐
Understand environmental, social, political, economic,
    or business systems . . . . ✓ ☐
Oversee and correct system performance . . . . ☐ ✓
Improve and create systems . . . . ☐ ✓

Technology:
Select technology . . . . ✓ ☐
Apply technology to task . . . . ✓ ☐
Maintain and troubleshoot technology . . . . . ✓ ☐

Foundation Skills

Basic Skills:
Read . . . . ✓ ☐
Write . . . . ✓ ☐
Do arithmetic and math . . . . ✓ ☐
Speak and listen . . . . ✓ ☐

Thinking Skills:
Learn . . . . ✓ ☐
Reason . . . . ✓ ☐
Think creatively . . . . ✓ ☐
Make decisions . . . . ✓ ☐
Solve problems . . . . ✓ ☐

Personal Qualities:
Take individual responsibility . . . . ✓ ☐
Have self-esteem and self-management . . . . . ✓ ☐
Be sociable . . . . ✓ ☐
Be fair, honest, and sincere . . . . ✓ ☐

must know how different materials and shapes work together.

Mechanical drafters who work on CAD systems must know how to use computers. They also need to understand manual drafting skills. These skills are useful even when using CAD programs. Drafters sometimes have to make drawings without computers.

General Knowledge

Mechanical drafters must keep up with the latest engineering technology. The CAD software and hardware systems change about every two years. Drafters may need to learn to use new computer programs and computer equipment.

Mechanical drafters also must understand manufacturing processes and technology. Changes occur often in manufacturing. Mechanical drafters must keep up to date on current technology. They must understand how machines and products are built. They must use this knowledge to create exact drawings.

Chapter 4

Preparing for the Career

Employers prefer mechanical drafters who have completed training after high school. People who want to become mechanical drafters need skills in math, science, basic drafting concepts, and computer-assisted drafting.

High School Education

Students who want to be mechanical drafters should take a variety of high school courses. For example, they should take math and science courses. Students learn how to do advanced calculations in math courses such as algebra and geometry. Students learn how different materials react together in science classes such as chemistry and physics. Some high schools also offer

Students who want to become mechanical drafters should enjoy math.

drafting courses where students can learn basic design and drafting concepts.

English and computer courses also are helpful. Students learn communication skills in English classes. Students learn how to use computers and different computer programs in computer classes.

High school students may gain experience through jobs after school or on weekends. They may work part-time at companies that employ mechanical drafters. Students may help with office work or do other such tasks. At these jobs, students can see how drafters work. Students also can meet with drafters. They can ask questions and tour drafters' work areas.

Post-Secondary Education

People who want to be mechanical drafters must attend a vocational school, technical school, or community college. In the United States, many of these schools offer an associate's degree in drafting.

Students take courses in drafting, math, science, and English. They learn basic drafting skills and how to work on CAD systems.

In the United States, mechanical drafting students can take an assessment test. Students can

High school students may learn basic drafting skills in drafting classes.

take this test at many technical and vocational schools. The test determines students' abilities in certain subject areas. The test results help determine which classes students should take.

In Canada, students may receive a drafting technology diploma from a community college or technical school. Students may complete a technician program in two years or a technologist program in three years.

A drafting technologist program prepares students to be more involved in design than a drafting technician program. Drafting technicians are less involved with the original design of objects than drafting technologists. Drafting technicians prepare engineering drawings. Drafting technologists develop and prepare engineering drawings from sketches, engineering measurements, and other data.

Certification

Mechanical drafters can work in the field after they successfully complete a drafting program. They do not need to be certified to work. But mechanical drafters may benefit from being certified. Employers know that certified mechanical drafters have a full understanding of the profession. Some employers prefer to hire certified mechanical drafters.

In the United States, mechanical drafters may take the Drafter Certification Test through the American Design Drafting Association (ADDA). This nationwide test program determines drafters' knowledge of drafting

Mechanical drafters can work in the field after they complete training.

concepts and national standards and practices. ADDA developed the test to elevate the profession's standards.

In Canada, mechanical drafters may obtain certificates of qualification through provincial associations. Mechanical drafters' certification may transfer from one province to another.

Chapter 5

The Market

Mechanical drafters need training and experience to get drafting jobs. Employers especially want to hire drafters with CAD system training.

Most drafters work for private companies. These drafters often work for engineering firms and manufacturing companies. Some drafters work for federal, state, provincial, or local governments.

Salary

Mechanical drafters' salaries depend on several factors. Drafters with more education usually earn more money to start. Drafters also earn more as they gain experience and acquire more skills. They often earn more money for jobs that have greater responsibilities.

It is beneficial for mechanical drafters to have CAD system training.

Salaries for mechanical drafters vary in the United States and Canada. In the United States, drafters earn between $19,000 and $50,750 per year. In Canada, drafters earn between $22,600 and $56,600 per year.

Job Outlook

The need for mechanical drafters will continue to grow in the future. Drafters will be needed by manufacturers, utility companies, and governments. In the United States, the job opportunities for mechanical drafters are expected to have average growth. In Canada, the job market is expected to remain fair.

Mechanical drafters may have more job opportunities when a country's economy is good. Manufacturers then may have more money to build new products. These companies will need drafters to create drawings for new products.

Advancement Opportunities

Mechanical drafters advance as they gain experience. Drafters improve their skills as they create drawings. With experience, drafters

Mechanical drafters may advance in their careers as they gain experience.

may earn promotions to higher levels within companies. For example, a Level 1 drafter may be moved to a Level 2 or Level 3 position. A drafter with several years of experience may become a drafting supervisor.

Some mechanical drafters start their own drafting businesses. They sell their services to

Some mechanical drafters become teachers.

companies that do not have drafters.
Some companies with drafting departments
may have too much work for their own
departments. They then hire independent
drafting companies to do the work.

Some mechanical drafters become teachers.
They may teach drafting at high schools,
technical schools, vocational schools, or
community colleges. These drafters may need
to return to school to earn teaching degrees.

Related Careers

People interested in mechanical drafting have a variety of job opportunities. Some drafters work in the architectural industry. Other people may become architects. Architects design buildings and other structures.

Some people interested in mechanical drafting may become engineers. These people design machinery, construct buildings and highways, and develop new products. Some engineers also test the products' quality.

Many jobs related to mechanical drafting require a bachelor's degree from a college or university. It usually takes people about four years to earn a bachelor's degree.

Mechanical drafters are an important part of manufacturing and engineering industries. Drafters will continue to be needed as new products are developed and technology advances. These mechanical drafters will help change older products or build new ones.

Words to Know

CAD (KAD)—short for computer-assisted or computer-aided drafting; the process of making drawings on a computer.

detail (di-TAYL)—additional information about an item on a drawing

dimension (duh-MEN-shuhn)—the measurements of an object; dimensions may be length, width, or height.

electronic (i-lek-TRON-ik)—something that is powered by small amounts of electricity; electronics include computers, TVs, and radios.

manufacturer (man-yuh-FAK-chur-ur)—a person or company that makes products

mechanical (muh-KAN-uh-kuhl)—having to do with machines or tools

specification (spess-uh-fuh-KAY-shuhn)— detailed engineering information and instructions about something that is to be built or made

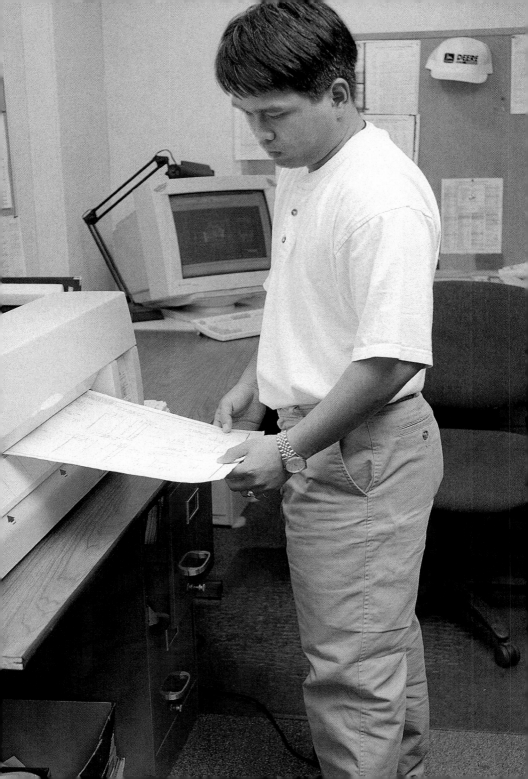

To Learn More

Bethune, James D. *Introduction to Electrical-Mechanical Drafting with CAD.* Upper Saddle River, N.J.: Prentice Hall, 1997.

Brown, Walter Charles. *Drafting for Industry.* South Holland, Ill.: Goodheart-Willcox, 1995.

Cosgrove, Holli, ed. *Career Discovery Encyclopedia.* Vol. 3. Chicago: Ferguson Publishing, 2000.

Rowh, Mark. *Opportunities in Drafting Careers.* VGM Opportunities. Lincolnwood, Ill.: VGM Career Horizons, 1994.

Young Person's Occupational Outlook Handbook. 2d ed. Indianapolis: JIST Works, 1999.

Useful Addresses

American Design Drafting Association
P.O. Box 11937
Columbia, SC 29211

Association for Career and Technical Education
1410 King Street
Alexandria, VA 22314

Canadian Vocational Association
P.O. Box 3435
Station D
Ottawa, ON K1P 6L4
Canada

Vocational Industrial Clubs of America
P.O. Box 3000
Leesburg, VA 20177-0300

Internet Sites

American Design Drafting Association
http://www.adda.org

Career Awareness—Draftsperson
http://hrdc-drhc.gc.ca/career/directions98/
eng/draft.shtml

Drafting/Design
http://www.deanza.fhda.edu/DeAnzaATC/
drafting.html

The Engineering Zone
http://www.flinthills.com/~ramsdale/EngZone/
design.htm

**Job Futures—Drafting Technologists and
Technicians**
http://www.hrdc-drhc.gc.ca/JobFutures/english/
volume1/2253/2253.htm

Occupational Outlook Handbook—Drafters
http://stats.bls.gov/oco/ocos111.htm

Index

advancement, 38–40
architectural industry, 8, 41
assessment test, 32–33

bachelor's degree, 41

certification, 34–35
checkers, 17
computer-assisted drafting (CAD), 12, 13, 15, 29, 32, 37

designers, 8, 11, 21

education, 31–33
engineers, 8–9, 10, 11, 12, 17, 20, 21, 25, 27, 41

Level 1 drafter, 19, 39
Level 2 drafter, 19, 39
Level 3 drafter, 19, 39
Level 4 drafter, 19

outlook, 38

plastics industry, 21
plotter, 13, 17, 23
project engineers, 9, 11, 20

salary, 37–38
supervisor, 15, 20–21, 26, 39

three-dimensional drawing, 23–24
two-dimensional drawing, 23–24